Baby Deer

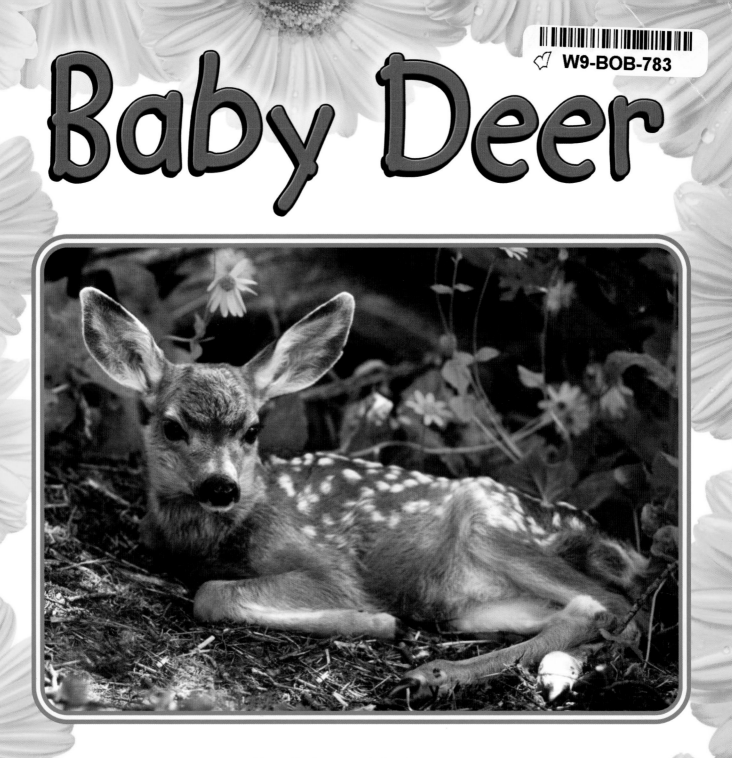

Bobbie Kalman

Crabtree Publishing Company
www.crabtreebooks.com

It's fun to
learn about
Baby Animals

Created by Bobbie Kalman

For baby Ava MacGregor,
a beautiful gift for Kathy and Rob.
We look forward to your arrival.

Author and
Editor-in-Chief
Bobbie Kalman

Editor
Robin Johnson

Photo research
Crystal Sikkens

Design
Katherine Berti
Samantha Crabtree (cover)

Production coordinator
Katherine Berti

Illustrations
Barbara Bedell: page 10 (bottom)
Katherine Berti: pages 7, 10 (top), 15, 24

Photographs
© iStockphoto.com: back cover (except background),
  pages 5, 11 (bottom), 20 (top)
© Shutterstock.com: front cover and background,
  pages 1 (background), 3, 4, 6, 7, 8 (inset),
  9 (inset), 10, 11 (top), 13, 14, 16, 17 (top),
  18, 19, 20 (bottom), 21 (top), 22, 23,
  24 (all except top right and bottom right)
Other images by Corbis, Corel, Creatas, and
  Digital Stock

Library and Archives Canada Cataloguing in Publication

Kalman, Bobbie, 1947-
    Baby deer / Bobbie Kalman.

(It's fun to learn about baby animals)
Includes index.
ISBN 978-0-7787-3952-4 (bound).--ISBN 978-0-7787-3971-5 (pbk.)

1. Fawns--Juvenile literature. I. Title. I. Series.

QL737.U55K34 2008   j599.6513'9   C2008-900468-X

Library of Congress Cataloging-in-Publication Data

Kalman, Bobbie.
  Baby deer / Bobbie Kalman.
      p. cm. -- (It's fun to learn about baby animals)
  Includes index.
  ISBN-13: 978-0-7787-3971-5 (pbk. : alk. paper)
  ISBN-10: 0-7787-3971-6 (pbk. : alk. paper)
  ISBN-13: 978-0-7787-3952-4 (reinforced library binding : alk. paper)
  ISBN-10: 0-7787-3952-X (reinforced library binding : alk. paper)
  1. Deer--Juvenile literature. 2. Fawns--Juvenile literature. I. Title. II. Series.
  QL737.U55K36 2008
  599.65'139--dc22
                                      2008002441

Crabtree Publishing Company

www.crabtreebooks.com   1-800-387-7650

Printed in the U.S.A./062011/SN20110520

Published in Canada
Crabtree Publishing
616 Welland Ave.
St. Catharines, Ontario
L2M 5V6

Published in the United States
Crabtree Publishing
PMB 59051
350 Fifth Avenue, 59th Floor
New York, New York 10118

Published in the United Kingdom
Crabtree Publishing
Maritime House
Basin Road North, Hove
BN41 1WR

Published in Australia
Crabtree Publishing
386 Mt. Alexander Rd.
Ascot Vale (Melbourne)
VIC 3032

What is in this book?

What is a deer?   4

Big and small deer   6

Meet more deer!   8

Deer bodies   10

Baby deer coats   12

All about antlers   14

What do deer eat?   16

Where do deer live?   18

Mother and baby   20

Growing up   22

Words to know
and Index   24

What is a deer?

A deer is a **mammal**. Mammals are animals with hair or fur. Deer have brown or gray hair covering their bodies. Mammal babies are born. Baby deer are born. You were born, too. You are a mammal.

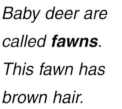

*Baby deer are called **fawns**. This fawn has brown hair.*

Mammal mothers make milk inside their bodies. Mammal babies drink the milk. Drinking mother's milk is called **nursing**. This fawn is nursing.

Big and small deer

There are many kinds of deer.
Deer are not all the same size. Some
deer are very big. Other deer are small.

This deer is a moose. It is the largest kind of deer.

This deer is a southern pudu. It is the smallest kind of deer.

moose

A moose is much bigger and heavier than a pudu is.

pudu

Meet more deer!

White-tailed deer, mule deer, and elk all live in North America. White-tailed deer are also called whitetails. Mule deer are named after **mules**. Mules are horses with big ears.

tail is up

tail is down

White-tailed deer are medium-sized deer. Their tails are white underneath.

Mule deer are bigger than whitetails. They have very large ears.

elk calf

Elk are almost as large as moose.
This elk is a **bull**. A bull is a large male
elk or moose. The elk above is a **calf**.
A calf is a young elk or moose.

Deer bodies

antlers

Deer have long bodies, thin legs, and short tails. They have **hoofs** on their feet. Hoofs are hard coverings. Male deer also have **antlers**. To learn more about antlers, see pages 14 and 15.

Both male and female moose have **dewlaps**. A dewlap is loose skin that is covered by hair.

Deer have short tails.

Deer have short hair on their bodies.

Deer have eyes on the sides of their heads. They can see almost all the way around their bodies.

toes

Deer have hard hoofs made of **horn**. Each hoof has two toes.

← Deer have → four thin legs.

hoofs →

10

Deer are vertebrates

Deer are **vertebrates**.
Vertebrates are animals with
backbones. Backbones are
the bones in the middle of an
animal's back. A vertebrate has many
other bones inside its body, too. All the
bones make up the animal's **skeleton**.

*A deer can
bend its legs.
It can run
and jump.*

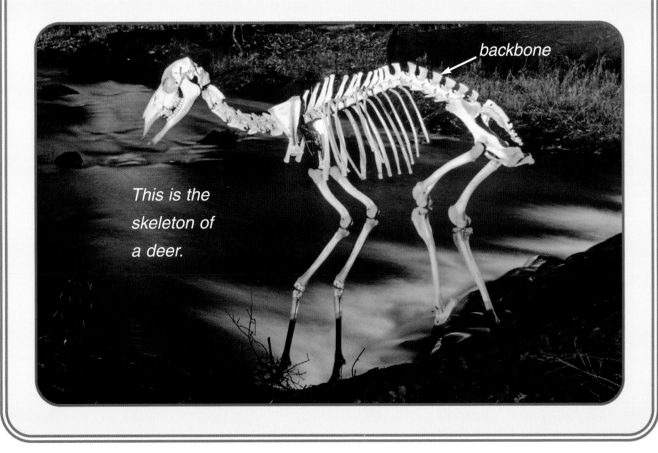

backbone

*This is the
skeleton of
a deer.*

Baby deer coats

Fawns have **patterns** of spots on their coats. The spots are **camouflage** for the fawns. Camouflage is colors or patterns that help an animal blend in with the world around it. Spots allow fawns to blend into the ground or into fields of flowers. The fawns are then hidden from **predators**. Predators are animals that hunt and eat other animals.

All about antlers

Bucks, or male deer, have antlers. Most female deer do not have antlers. Antlers are made of bone. Each year, old antlers fall off and new antlers grow. When the antlers start to grow, they are covered in soft skin called **velvet**. The antlers of this buck are covered in velvet.

This moose is rubbing the velvet off its antlers. The velvet will soon fall off.

The shiny antler on this moose is no longer covered in velvet.

A year of antlers

Spring

Antlers start growing in late spring.

Summer

The antlers are fully grown and are covered in velvet.

Fall

The buck rubs off the velvet. The bone shows through.

Winter

The antlers fall off one at a time.

15

What do deer eat?

Deer eat plants. Animals that eat mainly plants are called **herbivores**. Deer are herbivores called **browsers**. Browsers eat plant parts such as leaves and twigs.

These fawns have found some young plants to eat.

moose cow

moose calf

Most deer eat leaves, young plants, plants that grow in water, and small tree branches. The **cow** and her calf above are eating water plants. A cow is a large female moose or elk. This fawn is eating flowers. Flowers are soft and tasty foods for baby deer.

fawn

Where do deer live?

The natural places where animals live are called **habitats**. Some deer habitats are in very hot places. Others are in places that have cold winters. Many deer live in **forests** or near forests. Forests are habitats with many trees.

Forests have trees, bushes, and small young plants that deer like to eat.

Mule deer live at the edges of forests, where tall grasses grow.

Reindeer live in places with cold winters. These reindeer are looking for food under the snow.

Many deer visit people's back yards. They eat the plants that grow there.

Mother and baby

A mother deer visits her fawn often. The fawn cuddles with its mother.

After a fawn is born, its mother feeds it and takes it to a hiding place. The mother then leaves her baby. The fawn is safer on its own. Its spotted coat helps hide it from predators. The mother deer returns to feed the fawn several times each day.

This fawn is lying on the ground in a forest. It stays very still so predators will not see it.

Once the fawn is able to run well, it leaves its hiding place. It starts finding plants to eat with its mother. The fawn also nurses for a few more months.

The mother deer on the right is **grooming**, *or cleaning, her fawn.*

Growing up

As the fawn grows, it stops nursing and is able to find its own food. The fawn can live on its own, but it stays with its mother until she is ready to have another baby. When the fawn is about two years old, it is an adult deer. Adult deer can make babies.

This mother deer has twin fawns. Each baby started its **life cycle** when it was born. A life cycle is a set of changes in an animal's life. The fawns will grow and change until they become adults. As adults, they will make babies. With each baby, a new life cycle will begin.

Words to Know and Index

antlers

antlers
pages 10, 14–15

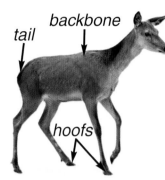
tail *backbone* *hoofs*

bodies
pages 4, 5, 10–11

pattern

coats
pages 12–13, 20

elk
pages 8, 9, 17

fawns
pages 4, 13,
16, 17, 20, 21,
22, 23

habitats
pages 18–19

moose
pages 6, 7, 9,
10, 15, 17

mule deer
pages 8, 19

southern pudu
page 7

white-tailed deer
page 8

Other index words
life cycle page 23
mammals pages 4, 5
nursing pages 5, 21, 22
plants pages 16–17, 18, 19, 21
reindeer page 19
vertebrates page 11